RECORDED VERSIONS
GUITAR

AUTHENTIC TRANSCRIPTIONS
WITH NOTES AND TABLATURE

BEST OF CARL Perkins

Cover photo: Michael Ochs / Michael Ochs Archives / Getty Images

ISBN 978-0-634-08494-2

HAL•LEONARD®
CORPORATION

7777 W. BLUEMOUND RD. P.O. BOX 13819 MILWAUKEE, WI 53213

Visit Hal Leonard Online at
www.halleonard.com

Blue Suede Shoes

Words and Music by Carl Lee Perkins

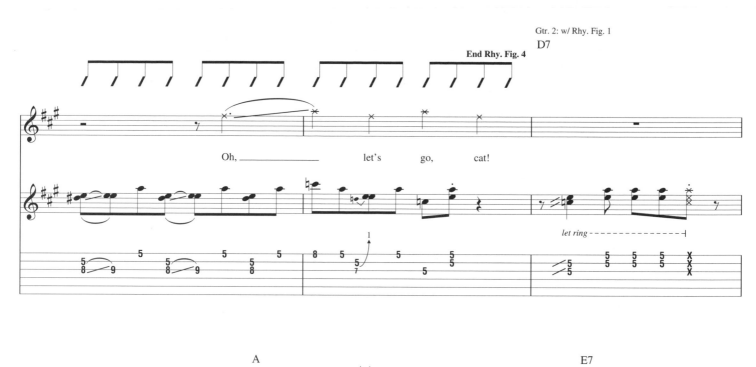

Oh, _____ let's go, cat!

3. Well, you can

Coda

Guitar Solo
Gtr. 2: w/ Rhy. Fig. 4

Rock!

7

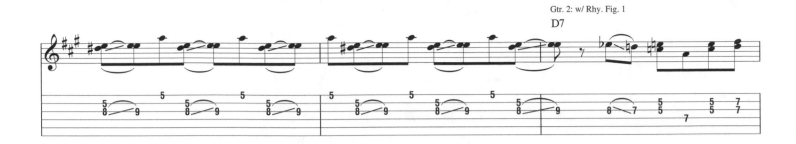

Verse

Gtr. 1: w/ Riff A
Gtr. 2: w/ Rhy. Fig 2

4. Well, it's one for the mon - ey, two for the show, three to get read - y, now

Gtr. 1: w/ Rhy. Fig. 3
Gtr. 2: w/ Rhy. Fig. 1

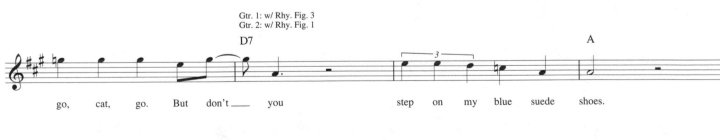

go, cat, go. But don't ___ you step on my blue suede shoes.

You can do an - y - thing, ___ but lay off ___ of my blue suede shoes.

Outro

Gtr. 2: w/ Rhy. Fig. 4

Well, it's... Blue, blue, blue suede shoes.

Gtr. 2: w/ Rhy. Fig. 1 (1st 6 meas.)

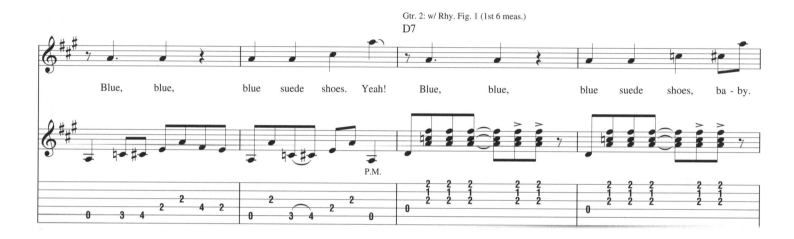

Blue, blue, blue suede shoes. Yeah! Blue, blue, blue suede shoes, ba - by.

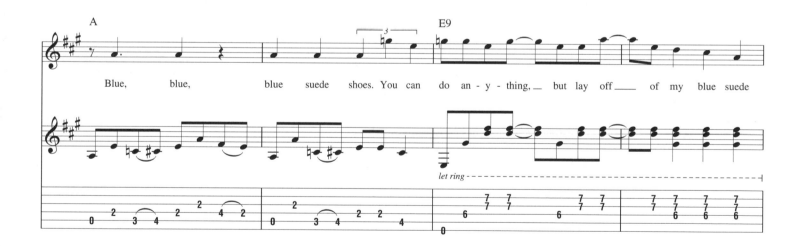

Blue, blue, blue suede shoes. You can do an - y - thing, __ but lay off __ of my blue suede

shoes.

from *Best of the Best*

Boppin' the Blues

Words and Music by Carl Lee Perkins and Howard Griffin

Verse

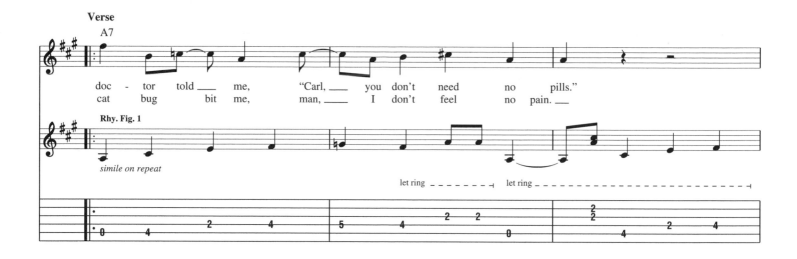

doc - tor told ___ me, "Carl, ___ you don't need no pills."
cat bug bit me, man, ___ I don't feel no pain. ___

simile on repeat

let ring ————— let ring ——————————————

Hey, ___ the doc - tor told ___ me, ___ "Boy, ___ you don't need no pills.
Yeah, ___ that jit-ter-bug caught me, ___ man, ___ I don't feel no pain. ___

let ring ——————— let ring ———————

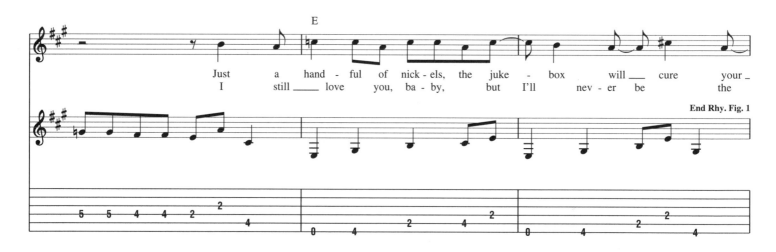

Just a hand - ful of nick - els, the juke - box will ___ cure your ___
I still ___ love you, ba - by, but I'll nev - er be the

End Rhy. Fig. 1

𝄋 Chorus

___ ills." ___ Well, all ___ my friends are bop - pin' the blues, ___ it
same. I said all my friends are bop - pin' the blues, ___ it
___ the cats are bop - pin' the blues, ___ and it

mf

simile on repeats

11

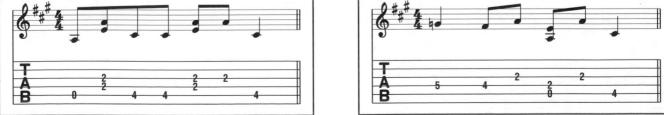

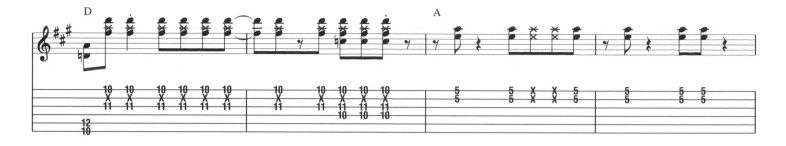

D.S. al Coda 1
(1st lyrics)

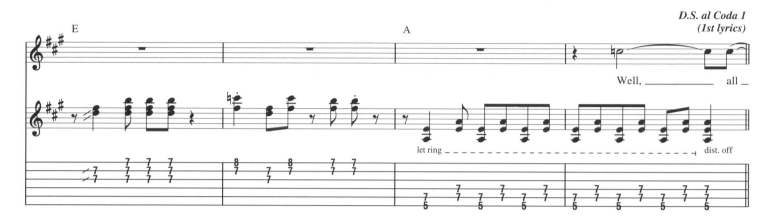

Well, _____ all _

Coda 1

Verse

3. Well, _____ Grand - pa done got rhy - thm and he

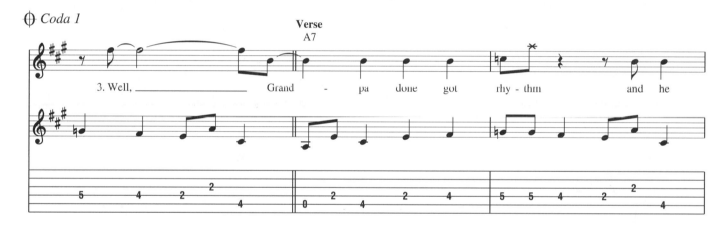

threw his crutch - es down. Oh, the old boy done got rhy - thm and blues _ and he

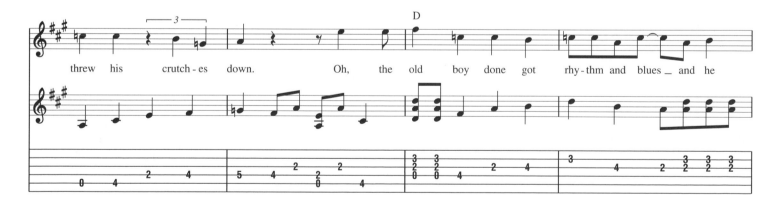

threw that crutch - es down. _ Grand - ma, he ain't _ tri -

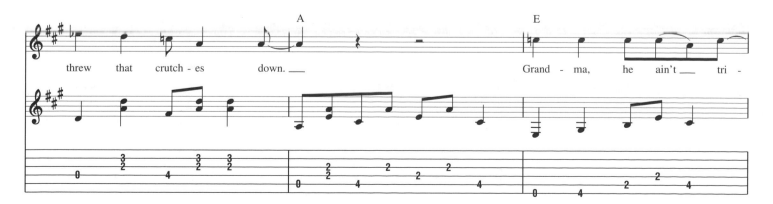

Dixie Fried

Words and Music by Carl Lee Perkins and Howard Griffin

*Chord symbols reflect overall harmony.

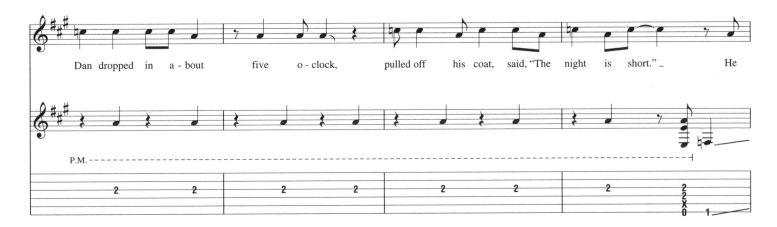

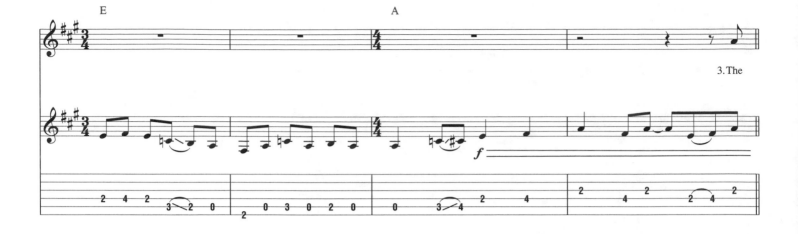

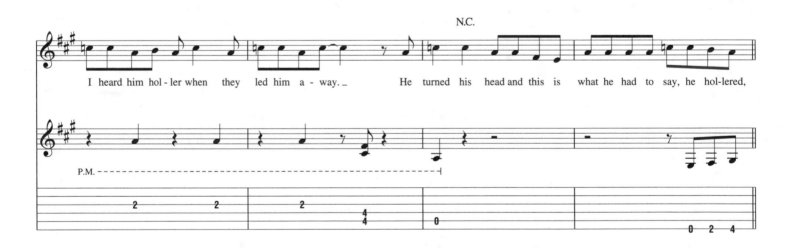

al - most dawn and the cops are gone. Let's all ____ get dix - ie fried." _ Get fried _ now.

Guitar Solo

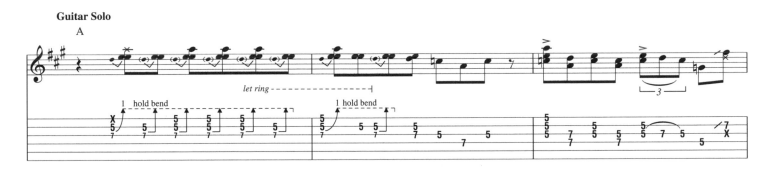

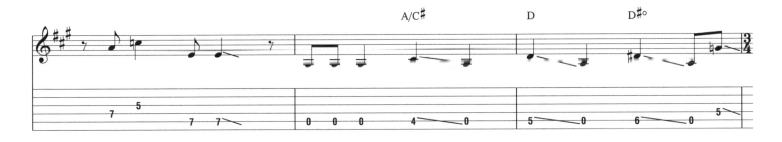

4. Now,

Verse

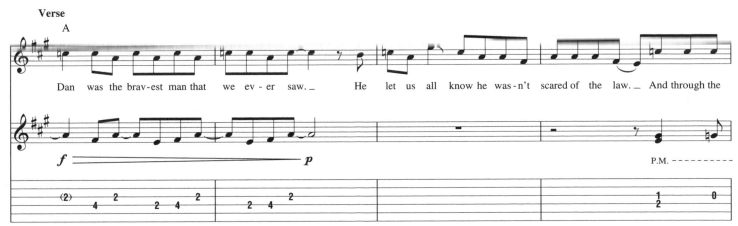

Dan was the brav-est man that we ev - er saw. _ He let us all know he was-n't scared of the law. _ And through the

Everybody's Trying to Be My Baby

Words and Music by Carl Lee Perkins

*Chord symbols reflect basic harmony.

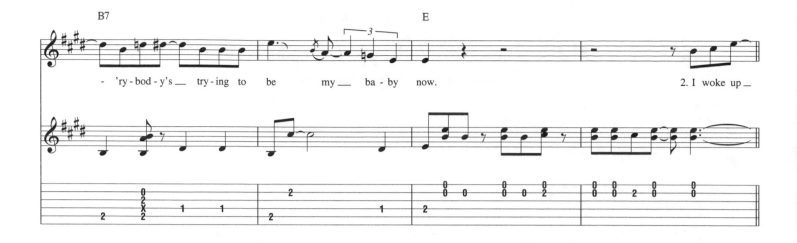

Verse

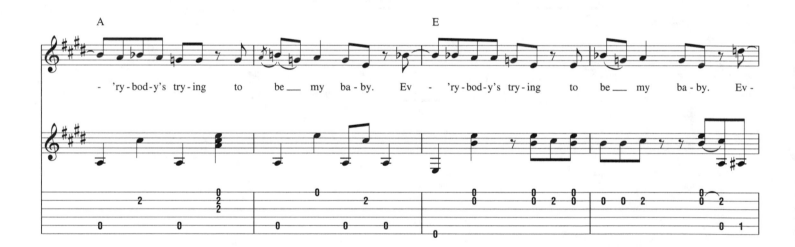

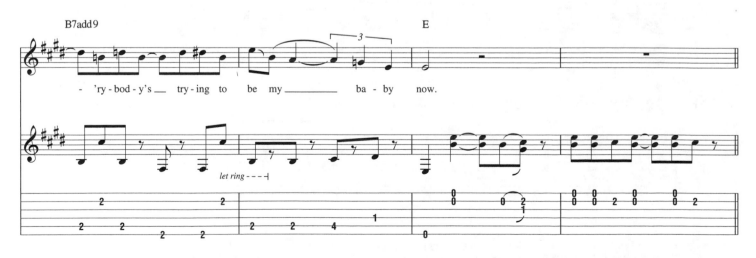

Guitar Solo

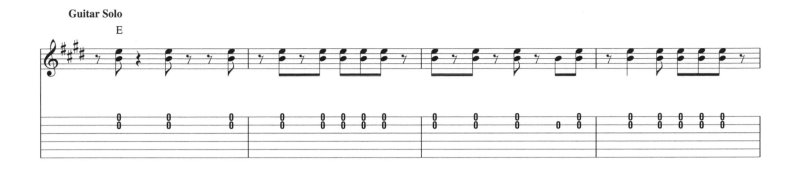

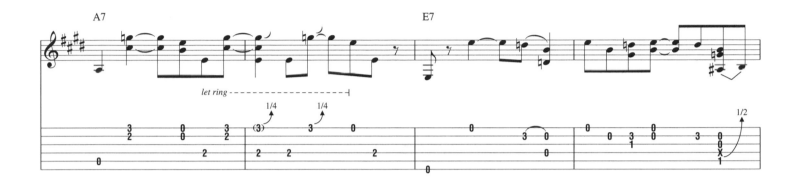

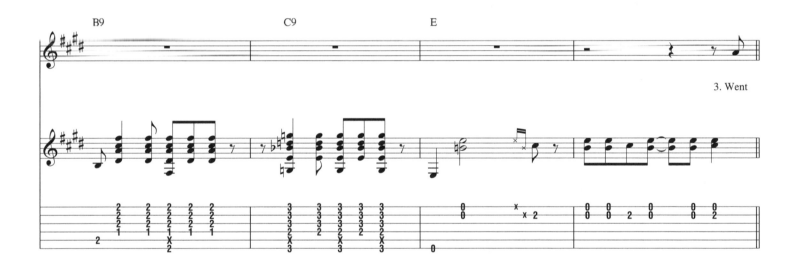

3. Went

Verse

out last night (did-n't) mean to stay late, (be-)fore home I had nine-teen_ dates. Ev -

-'ry-bod-y's __ try'n' to be __ my __ ba-by. Ev - 'ry-bod-y's __ try-ing to be __ my __ ba-by. Ev -

-'ry-bod-y's __ try-ing to be my ___ ba-by now.

let ring - - - -

Guitar Solo

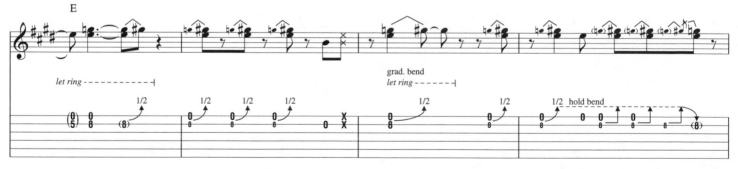

let ring - - - - - - - - - - -   *grad. bend*
                                        let ring - - - - - -

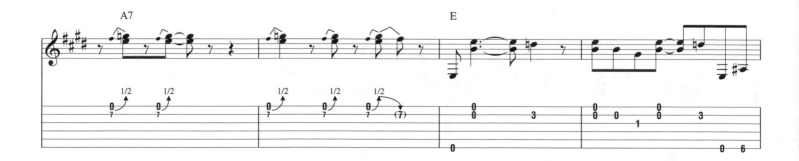

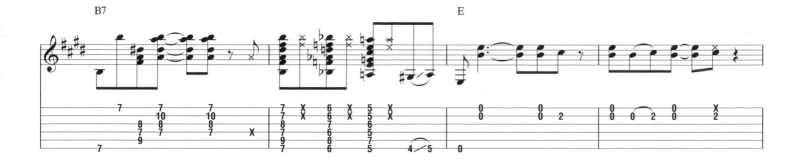

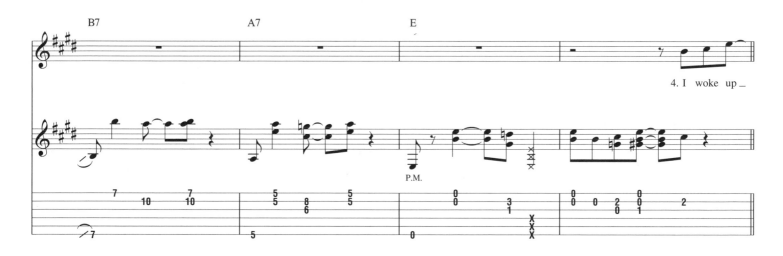

4. I woke up

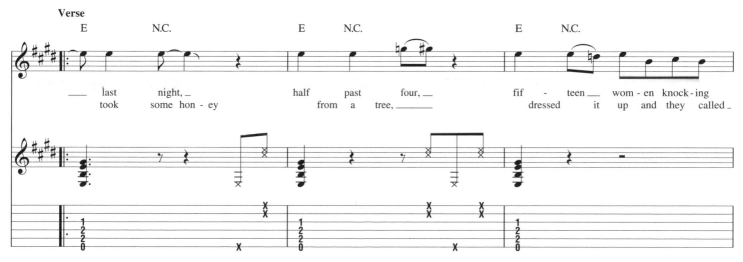

Verse

last night, ___ half past four, ___ fif - teen ___ wom - en knock - ing

took some hon - ey from a tree, ___ dressed it up and they called

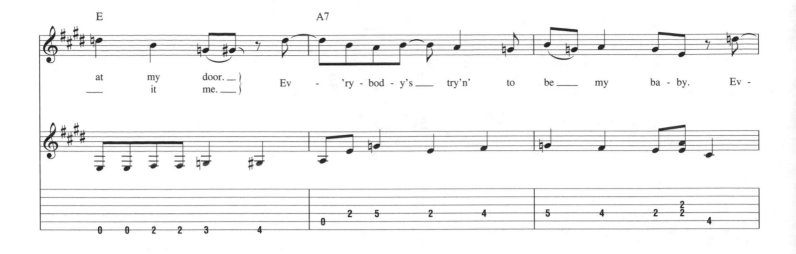

at my door. Ev - 'ry - bod - y's try'n' to be my ba - by. Ev-

it me.

- 'ry - bod - y's try - ing to be my ba - by. Ev - 'ry - bod - y's try - ing to

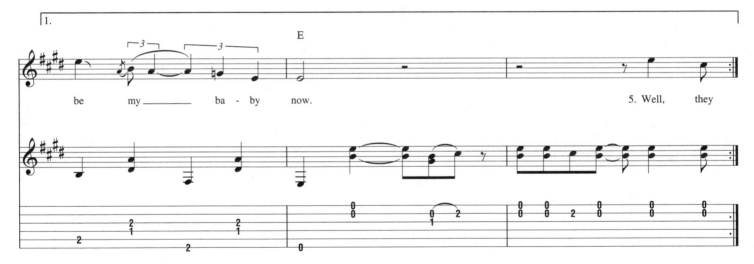

1.

be my ba - by now. 5. Well, they

2.

be my ba - by now.

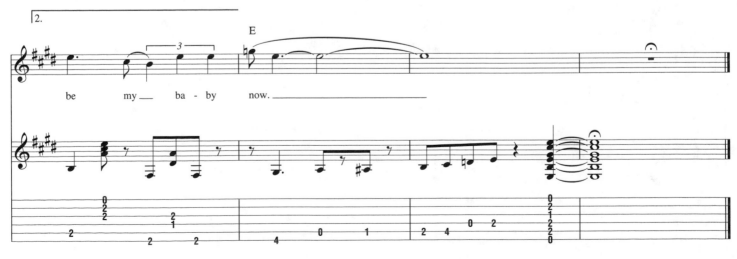

Glad All Over

Words and Music by Dave Clark and Mike Smith

*Chord symbols reflect overall harmony.

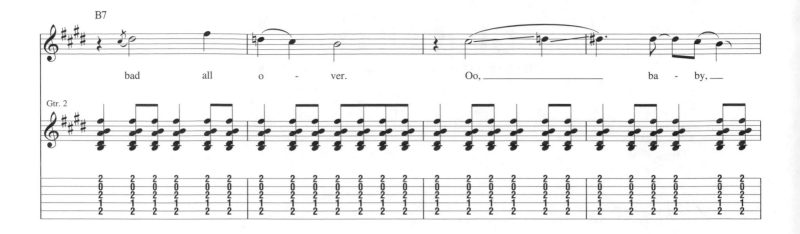

bad   all   o - ver.   Oo, _____   ba - by, ___

Gtr. 2

hot dang, dil - ly, so thrill - y, but I'm ___ glad all _____ o - ver. ___   2. I got

End Rhy. Fig. 1

Gtr. 2

Gtr. 1

Verse
Gtr. 2: w/ Rhy. Fig. 1

goose pim - ples, ba - by, 'cause it feels so good _ when you cud - dle me like you do, and I ___ feel

Gtr. 1

let ring -

Gtr. 1 tacet
B7

bad   all   o - ver.   Oo, _____   mer - cy.

Gone, Gone, Gone
Words and Music by Carl Lee Perkins

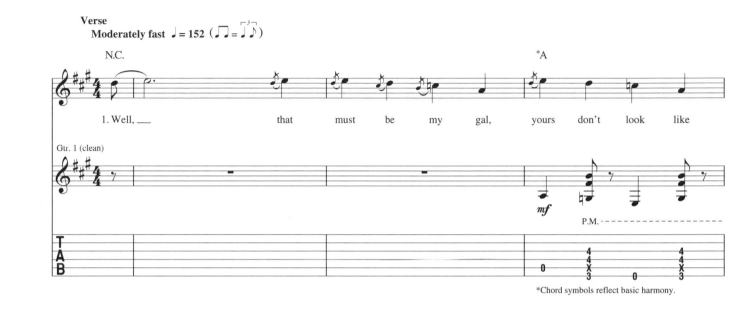

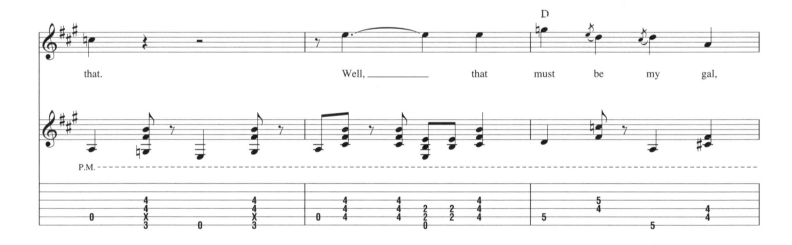

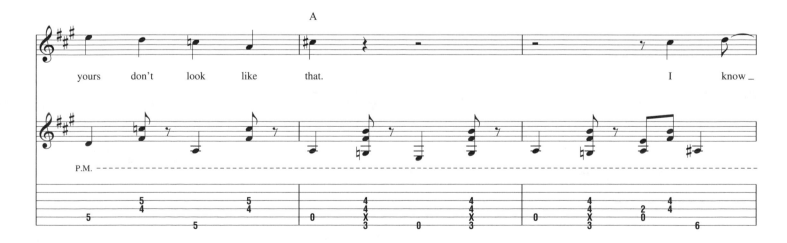

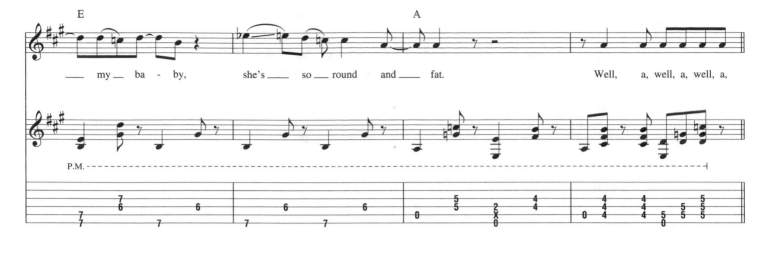

___ my ba - by, she's ___ so ___ round and ___ fat. Well, a, well, a, well, a,

Chorus

gone, ___ gone, ___ gone. ___ Gone, ___ gone, ___ gone. _ Well, I'm

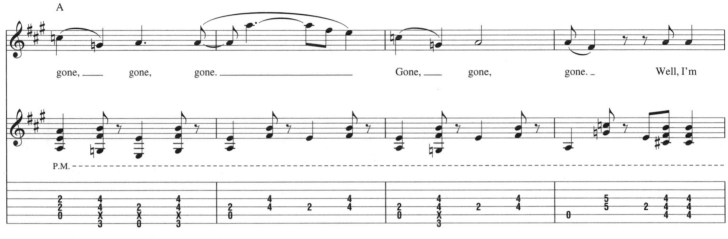

gone, ___ gone, ___ gone. Well, I'm gone, gone, gone. _ And I'm

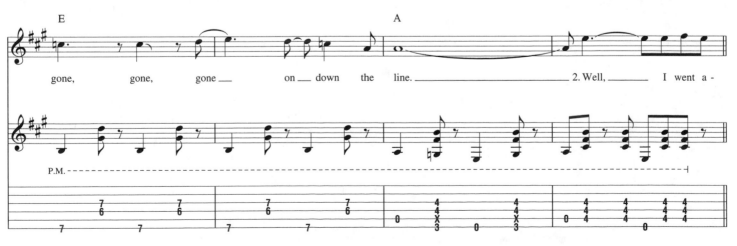

gone, gone, gone ___ on down the line. ___ 2. Well, ___ I went a -

Verse

round that square dance, ev-'ry-bod-y's jump-ing to - night. _____ Yeah, _____ I went a -

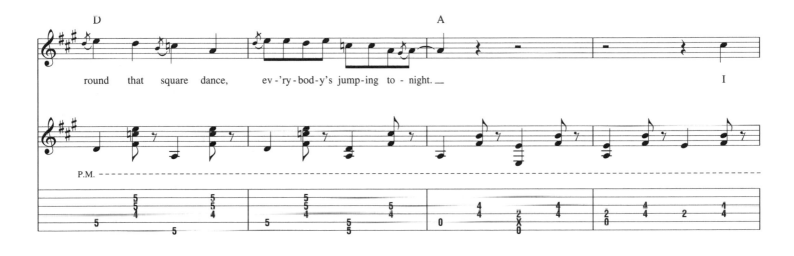

round that square dance, ev-'ry-bod-y's jump-ing to - night. _____ I

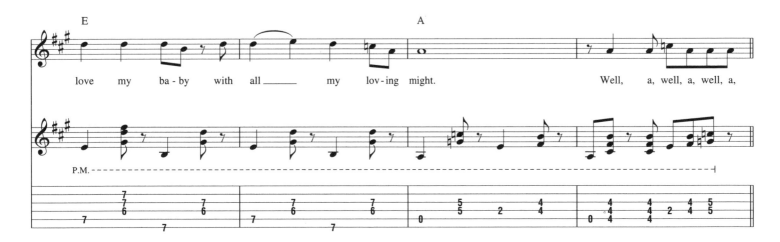

love my ba-by with all _____ my lov-ing might. Well, a, well, a, well, a,

Chorus

gone, _____ gone, gone, _____ buh, buh. Well, I'm gone, _____ gone, gone. _____ And I'm

Verse

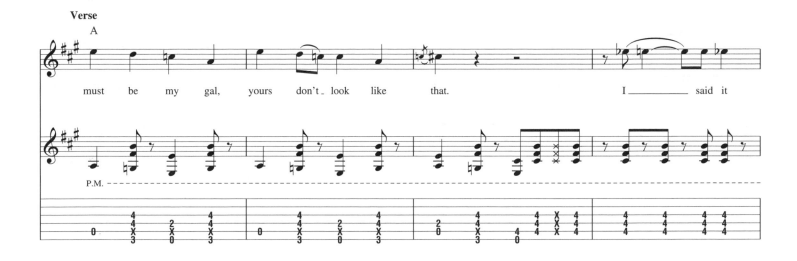

must be my gal, yours don't look like that. I _____ said it

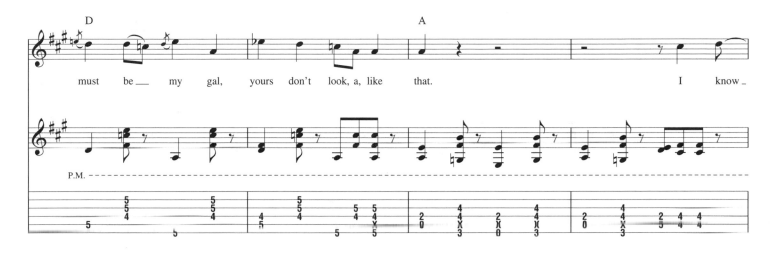

must be ___ my gal, yours don't look, a, like that. I know __

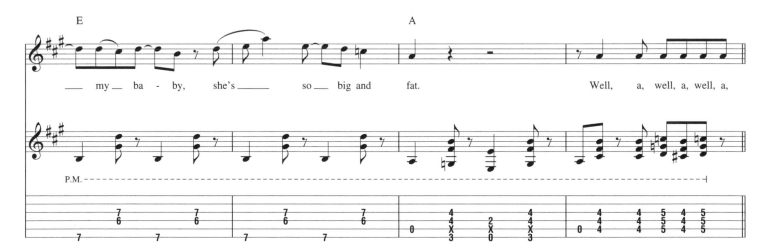

___ my ba - by, she's _____ so ___ big and fat. Well, a, well, a, well, a,

Chorus

gone, _____ gone, _____ gone. Well, a, ba - a - by, gone, _____ gone, _____ gone. _____ I'm __

gone, _____ gone, _ gone. ____ Hey, I'm gone, _____ gone, _ gone. ____ Well, I'm

gone, _ gone, ____ gone. ____ Come _ go with me. _____ Let's _ go now, _ now.

Guitar Solo

Wang, do, ma - ma, bop, ____ ba, bop, pa, fang, do, bop, pa, do, fang, do.

w/ pick & fingers

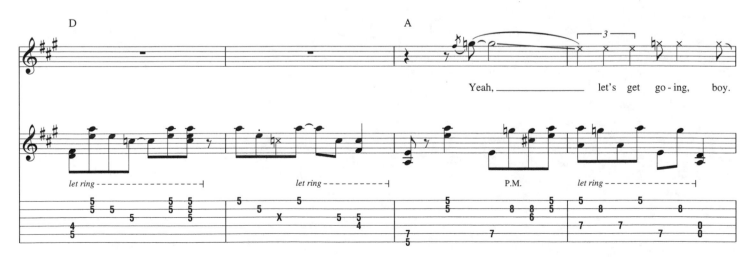

Yeah, _____ let's get go - ing, boy.

let ring ----------- let ring ----------- P.M. let ring -----------

38

Oh, _____ Whoa, ___ and I'm

Chorus

gone, gone, gone, ___ ba - by. But, well, a, gone, gone, gone. Well, _____ I'm

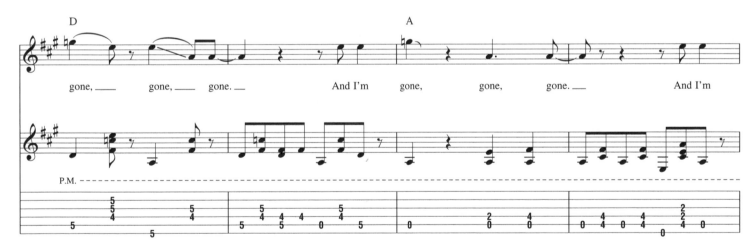

gone, ___ gone, ___ gone. ___ And I'm gone, gone, gone. ___ And I'm

gone, gone, gone. ___ Come go with me. ___

Honey Don't

Words and Music by Carl Lee Perkins

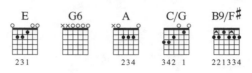

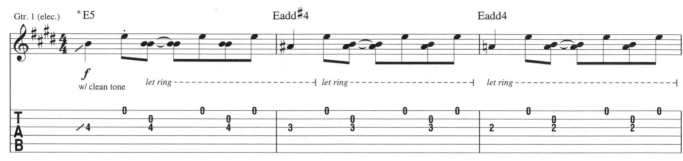

Intro
Moderately fast ♩ = 172

*Chord symbols reflect implied harmony.

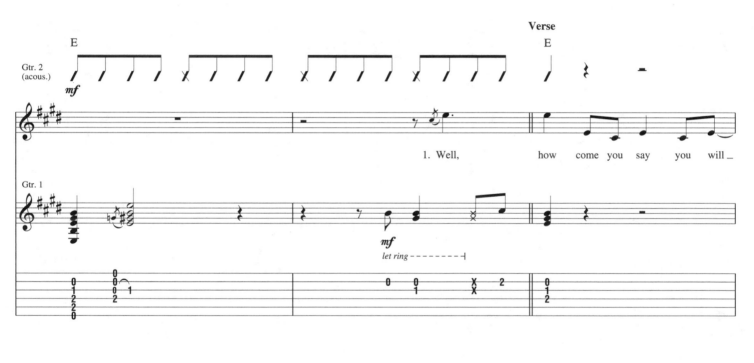

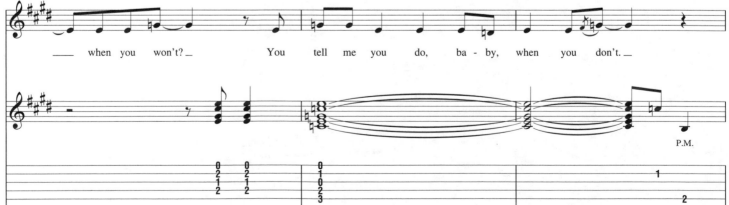

don't.   Hey, _____ hon-ey, don't   say you

will   when you won't.   Huh,   ah, _____ hon-ey, don't. ___   2. Well,   I

love   you   ba-by,   and you   ought   to   know___   I   like the   way   that you   wear   your   clothes.

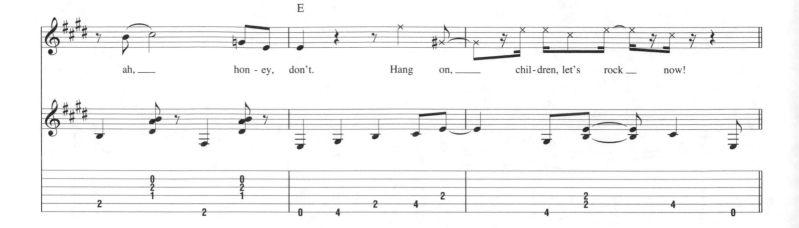

ah, ___ hon-ey, don't. Hang on, ___ chil-dren, let's rock ___ now!

Guitar Solo

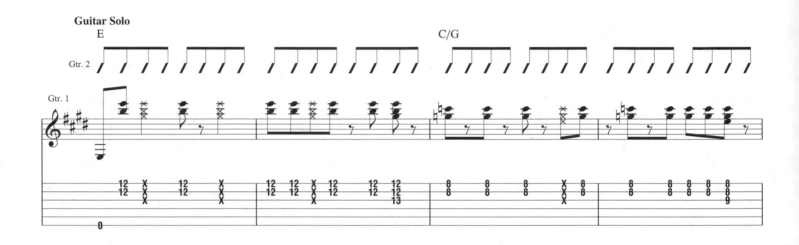

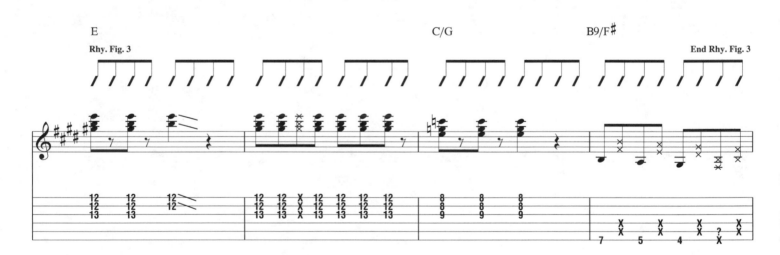

Gtr. 2: w/ Rhy. Fig. 2

Oh, ___ hon-ey, don't.

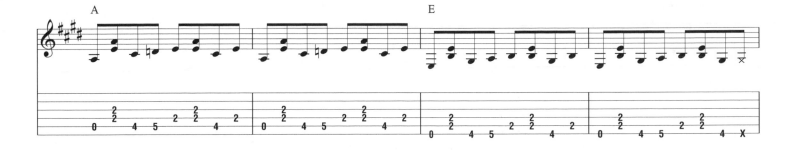

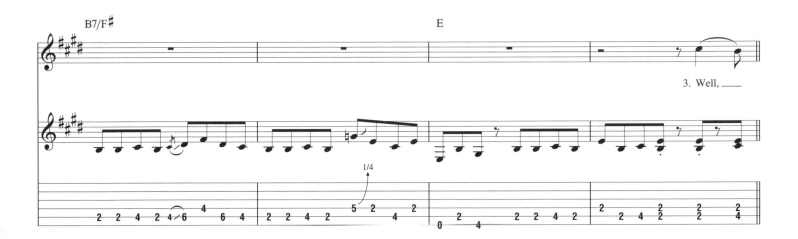

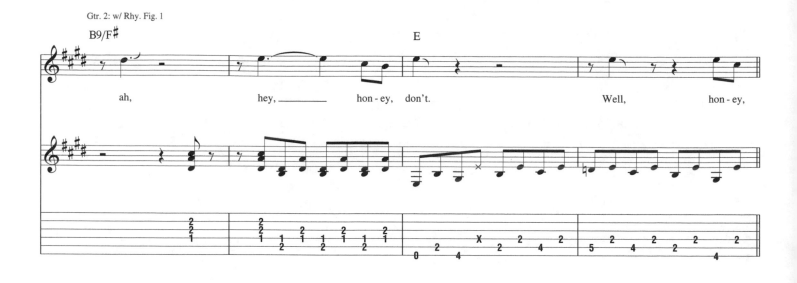

Gtr. 2: w/ Rhy. Fig. 1

B9/F#   E

ah,   hey, ___ hon-ey, don't.   Well,   hon-ey,

Chorus

Gtr. 2: w/ Rhy. Fig. 2

E

don't.   Bop,   bop,   bop, ___ hon-ey, don't. Bop,   bop,   bop,   bop, ___ hon-ey,

Gtr. 1: w/ Riff B   Gtr. 1: w/ Riff A

A   E

don't. ___   Well, ___ hon-ey, don't ___   say   you

B9/F#   E

will when you won't. Huh, ah,   hon-ey, don't. ___ Get it, cat. Let's ___ go   now! ___

Gtr. 1

Guitar Solo

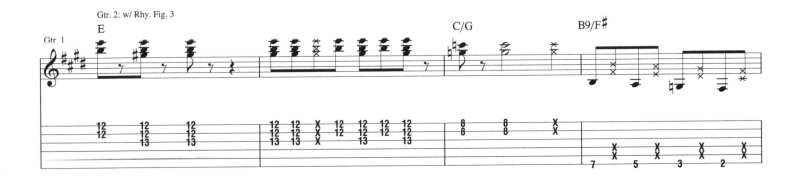

Chorus
Gtr. 2: w/ Rhy. Fig. 2 (1st 10 meas.)

don't. _____   Ho, _____   hon - ey,   don't. _____

Yeah, hon-ey, don't. Bop, bop, ba, bop, ba, bop,_ hon-ey, don't

say you will when you won't. Huh, ah,_ hon-ey, don't._

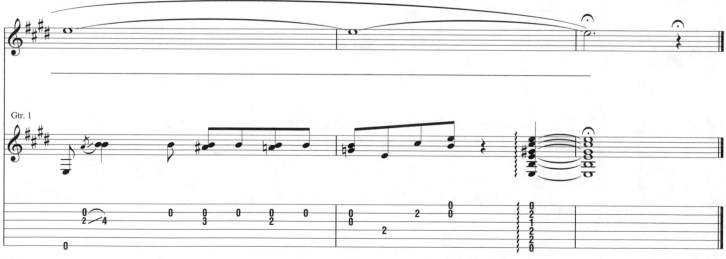

from *The Definitive Colletion*

Lend Me Your Comb

Words and Music by Fred Wise, Benjamin Weisman and Kathleen Twomey

Bridge

Gtr. 3: w/ Riff C
Gtr. 1: w/ Rhy. Fig. 2

Kiss-ing you __ was __ fun, __ hon-ey bun-ny. Thanks __ for the date.

Time has ___ come to ___ run, ___ hon-ey, but ___ sug-ar boog-er, it's, a, ___ a, get-ting late. ___

Verse

Gtr. 4: w/ Rhy. Fig. 1 (1st 6 meas.)

___ 3. Just wait till I (Huh.) straight-en my

from *Best of the Best*

Matchbox

Words and Music by Carl Lee Perkins

*Chord symbols reflect overall harmony.

*Gtr. 2: piano arr. for gtr.
**composite arrangement

got no match-es but I got a long way to go. 1. I'm an old,

Verse
Gtr. 2 tacet

poor boy, long way from home. I'm an old,

Gtr. 1 **Rhy. Fig. 1**

poor boy, long way from home. Guess I'll

nev-er been hap-py; ev-'ry thing I do is wrong. Yeah.

End Rhy. Fig. 1

Guitar Solo

Gtr. 3 (clean) Gtr. 1: w/ Rhy. Fig. 1, 1st 8 meas.

f

2. Well,

P.H. *loco* *8va*

pitch: B

Verse

Gtr. 1: w/ Rhy. Fig. 1
Gtr. 3 tacet

let me be your lit-tle dog _ till your big dog comes. _ Let me

be your lit-tle dog, ah, till your _ big dog _ comes. _ When the

big dog gets _ here, _ show him what this lit-tle pup-py done. _ Well, _____ I'm _ sit-

Put Your Cat Clothes On

By Carl Lee Perkins

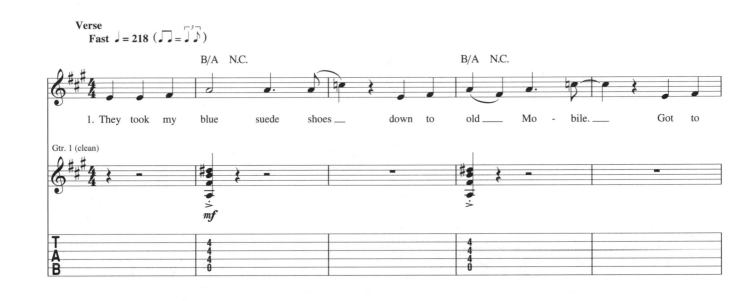

1. They took my blue suede shoes ___ down to old ___ Mo - bile. ___ Got to

rock - in' with the rhy - thm, run 'em o - ver at the hill. ___ Put your

cat clothes on ___ 'cause to - night we're gon - na real - ly rock ___ it right. ___

*Chord symbols reflect overall harmony.

Yeah, _____ kit - ty, put your
cat clothes __ on ___ 'cause to - night __ we're gon - na real - ly bop 'em right. __

𝄋 Verse

_____
2.Well, I _____ slicked up my - self __ till I,
come on, cat, get, a, with it, keep your hands __

I look like a ___ dil - ly.   I run down - town and get __ my _____
___ off that fruit jar.   Do some   be - bop - pin' rhy - thm,   pick the toe-

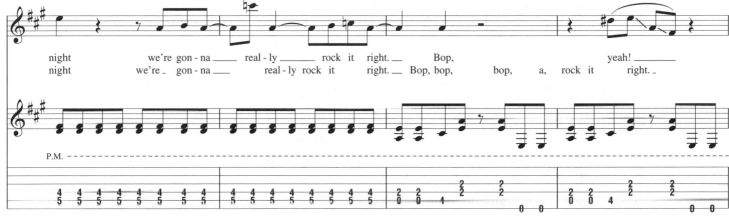

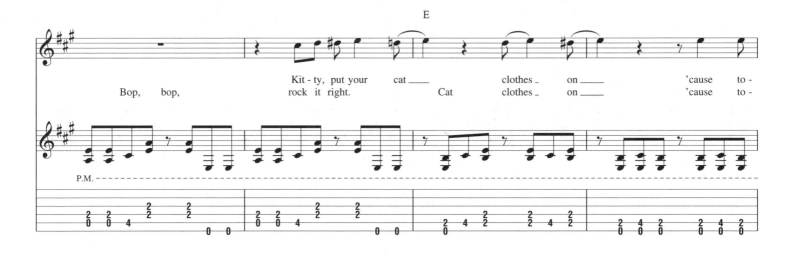

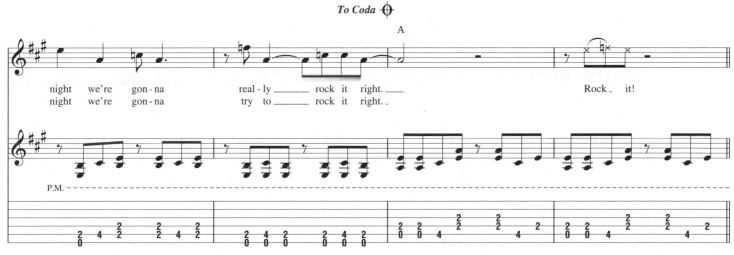

Piano Solo

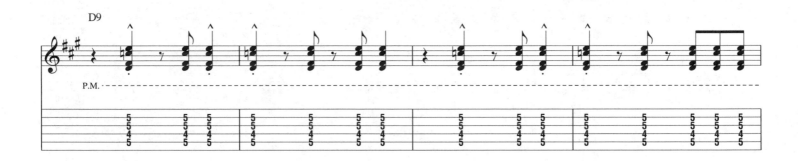

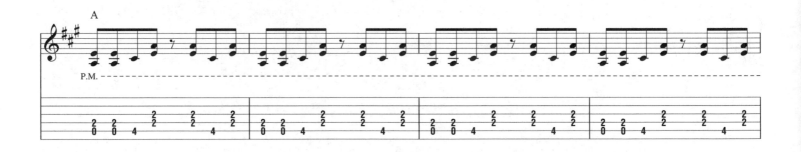

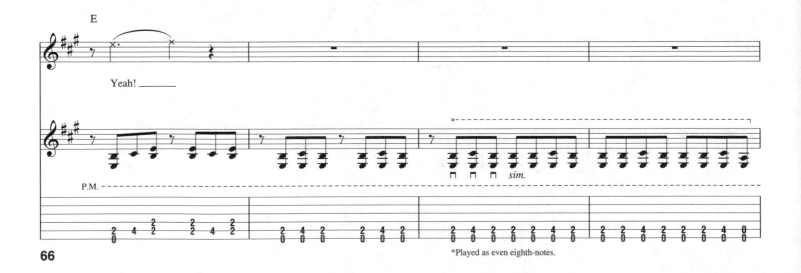

*Played as even eighth-notes.

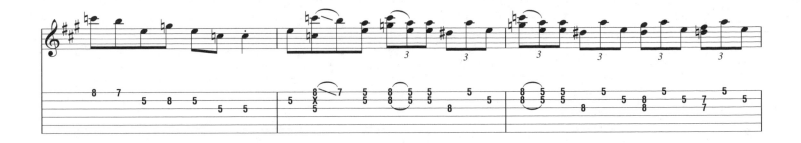

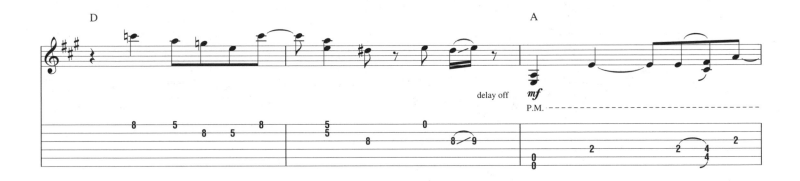

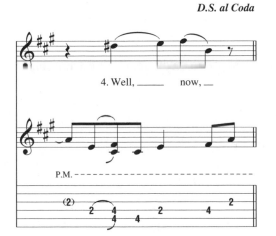

4. Well, _____ now, _____

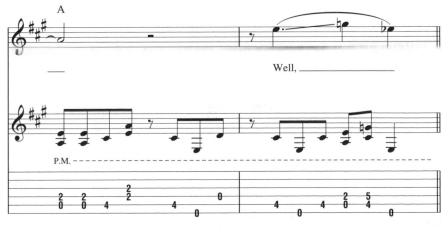

D.S. al Coda

Coda

A

_____ Well, _____

Outro

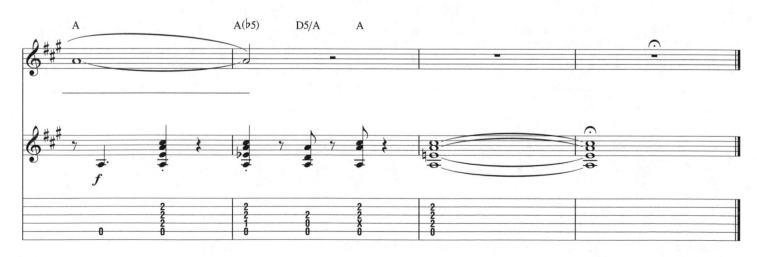

You Can't Make Love to Somebody (With Somebody Else on Your Mind)

Words and Music by Carl Lee Perkins

*Chord symbols reflect overall harmony.

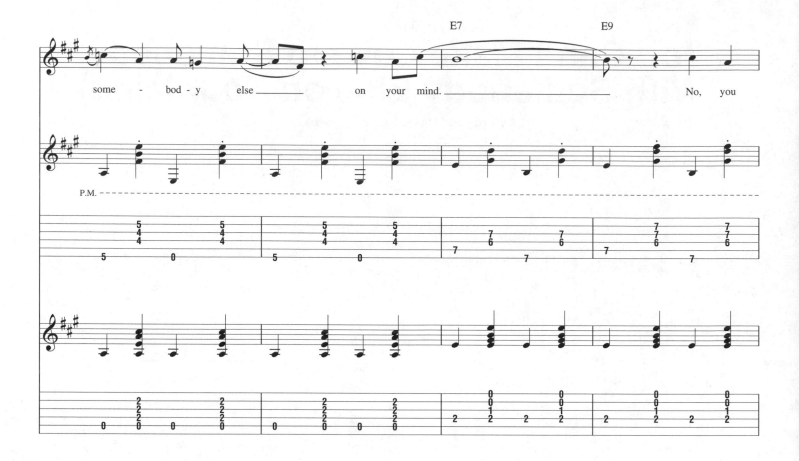

some - bod - y else _____ on your mind. _____ No, you

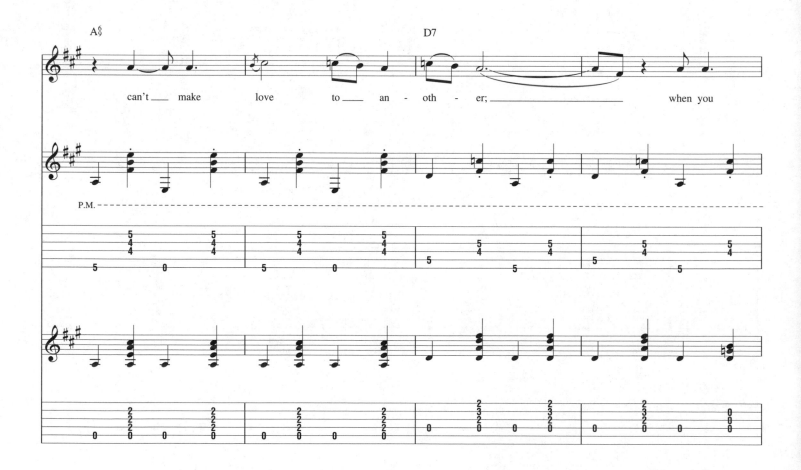

can't ___ make love to ___ an - oth - er; _____ when you

can't ___ make ___ love ___ to an - oth - er; _____ when you

try ___ you're just wast - ing your time. _____ Ba, bop, boop, bop,

Gtr. 2: w/ Rhy. Fill 1   Gtr. 2: w/ Rhy. Fig. 1 (last 3 meas.)

Guitar Solo
Gtr. 2: w/ Rhy. Fig. 1

bop, ba, da, bop, ba, da. Yeah. ___

Rhy. Fill 1
Gtr. 2

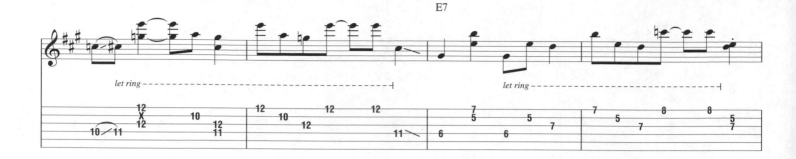

D.S. al Coda

2. I took my

Coda

Chorus

Gtr. 2: w/ Rhy. Fig. 1

can't, ___ a, make, a, love to some- bod- y _____ when you've got

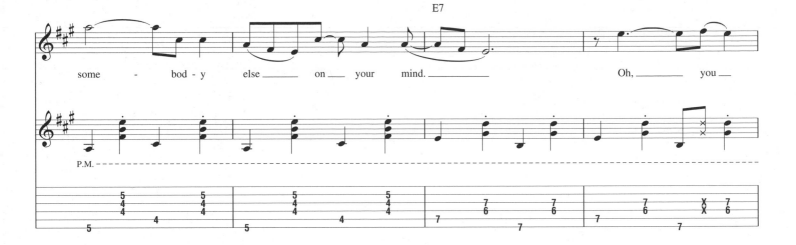

some - bod - y else ___ on ___ your mind. ___ Oh, ___ you ___

can't ___ make ___ love ___ to an - oth - er ___ and your

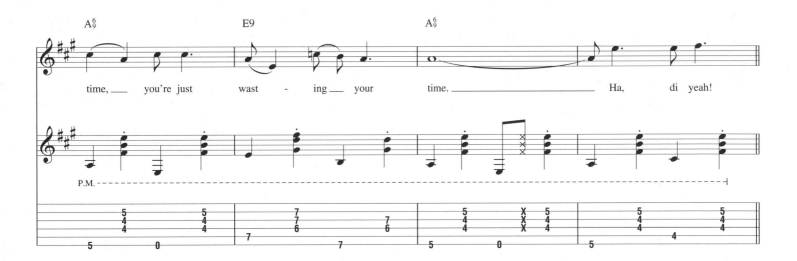

time, ___ you're just wast - ing ___ your time. ___ Ha, di yeah!

Guitar Solo
Gtr. 2; w/ Rhy. Fig. 1

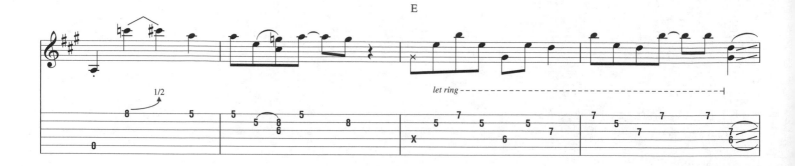

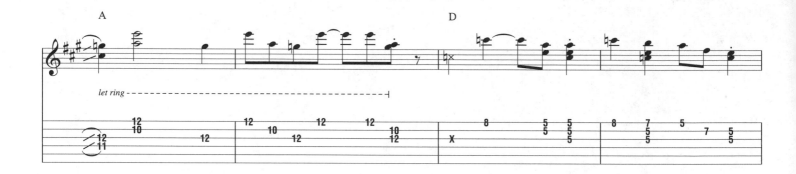

Well, a, well, a, well, a,   well, a, well, a, well,   you

Chorus

Gtr. 2: w/ Rhy. Fig. 1 (1st 14 meas.)

A_9^6

can't   make   love   to   some - bod - y   when   you've got

Your True Love

Words and Music by Carl Lee Perkins

Capo II

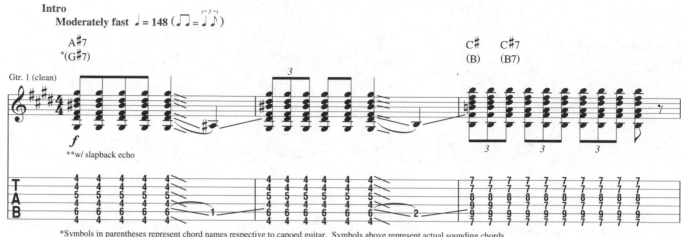

*Symbols in parentheses represent chord names respective to capoed guitar. Symbols above represent actual sounding chords.
Capoed fret is "0" in tab. Chord symbols reflect basic harmony.

**Set echo at approx. 91.9 ms delay.

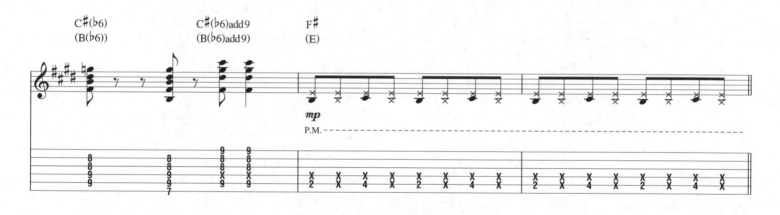

***Refers to upstemmed voc. only.

Chorus
Bkgd. Voc.: w/ Voc. Fig. 1 (3 times)
Gtr. 1: w/ Rhy. Fig. 1 (3 times)

Guitar Notation Legend

Guitar music can be notated three different ways: on a *musical staff*, in *tablature*, and in *rhythm slashes*.

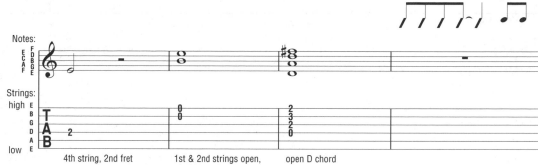

RHYTHM SLASHES are written above the staff. Strum chords in the rhythm indicated. Use the chord diagrams found at the top of the first page of the transcription for the appropriate chord voicings. Round noteheads indicate single notes.

THE MUSICAL STAFF shows pitches and rhythms and is divided by bar lines into measures. Pitches are named after the first seven letters of the alphabet.

TABLATURE graphically represents the guitar fingerboard. Each horizontal line represents a string, and each number represents a fret.

HALF-STEP BEND: Strike the note and bend up 1/2 step.

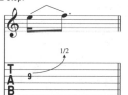

WHOLE-STEP BEND: Strike the note and bend up one step.

GRACE NOTE BEND: Strike the note and immediately bend up as indicated.

SLIGHT (MICROTONE) BEND: Strike the note and bend up 1/4 step.

BEND AND RELEASE: Strike the note and bend up as indicated, then release back to the original note. Only the first note is struck.

PRE-BEND: Bend the note as indicated, then strike it.

VIBRATO: The string is vibrated by rapidly bending and releasing the note with the fretting hand.

WIDE VIBRATO: The pitch is varied to a greater degree by vibrating with the fretting hand.

HAMMER-ON: Strike the first (lower) note with one finger, then sound the higher note (on the same string) with another finger by fretting it without picking.

PULL-OFF: Place both fingers on the notes to be sounded. Strike the first note and without picking, pull the finger off to sound the second (lower) note.

LEGATO SLIDE: Strike the first note and then slide the same fret-hand finger up or down to the second note. The second note is not struck.

SHIFT SLIDE: Same as legato slide, except the second note is struck.

TRILL: Very rapidly alternate between the notes indicated by continuously hammering on and pulling off.

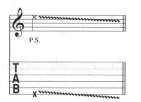

TAPPING: Hammer ("tap") the fret indicated with the pick-hand index or middle finger and pull off to the note fretted by the fret hand.

NATURAL HARMONIC: Strike the note while the fret-hand lightly touches the string directly over the fret indicated.

PINCH HARMONIC: The note is fretted normally and a harmonic is produced by adding the edge of the thumb or the tip of the index finger of the pick hand to the normal pick attack.

PICK SCRAPE: The edge of the pick is rubbed down (or up) the string, producing a scratchy sound.

MUFFLED STRINGS: A percussive sound is produced by laying the fret hand across the string(s) without depressing, and striking them with the pick hand.

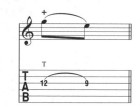

PALM MUTING: The note is partially muted by the pick hand lightly touching the string(s) just before the bridge.

RAKE: Drag the pick across the strings indicated with a single motion.

TREMOLO PICKING: The note is picked as rapidly and continuously as possible.

VIBRATO BAR DIVE AND RETURN: The pitch of the note or chord is dropped a specified number of steps (in rhythm), then returned to the original pitch.

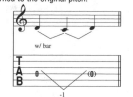

VIBRATO BAR SCOOP: Depress the bar just before striking the note, then quickly release the bar.

VIBRATO BAR DIP: Strike the note and then immediately drop a specified number of steps, then release back to the original pitch.

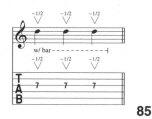

GUITAR RECORDED VERSIONS®

AUTHENTIC TRANSCRIPTIONS WITH NOTES AND TABLATURE

Guitar Recorded Versions® are note-for-note transcriptions of guitar music taken directly off recordings. This series, one of the most popular in print today, features some of the greatest guitar players and groups from blues and rock to country and jazz.

Guitar Recorded Versions are transcribed by the best transcribers in the business. Every book contains notes and tablature. Visit www.halleonard.com for our complete selection.

00690501 Bryan Adams – Greatest Hits $19.95
00690002 Aerosmith – Big Ones $24.95
00692015 Aerosmith – Greatest Hits $22.95
00690603 Aerosmith – O Yeah! (Ultimate Hits) $24.95
00690147 Aerosmith – Rocks....$19.95
00690139 Alice in Chains $19.95
00690178 Alice in Chains – Acoustic $19.95
00694865 Alice in Chains – Dirt....$19.95
00660225 Alice in Chains – Facelift $19.95
00694925 Alice in Chains – Jar of Flies/Sap $19.95
00690387 Alice in Chains – Nothing Safe: Best of the Box $19.95
00690899 All That Remains – The Fall of Ideals $19.95
00690812 All-American Rejects – Move Along $19.95
00694932 Allman Brothers Band – Definitive Collection for Guitar Volume 1 ....$24.95
00694933 Allman Brothers Band – Definitive Collection for Guitar Volume 2 ....$24.95
00694934 Allman Brothers Band – Definitive Collection for Guitar Volume 3 ....$24.95
00690755 Alter Bridge – One Day Remains $19.95
00690571 Trey Anastasio $19.95
00690158 Chet Atkins – Almost Alone $19.95
00694876 Chet Atkins – Contemporary Styles....$19.95
00694878 Chet Atkins – Vintage Fingerstyle $19.95
00690865 Atreyu – A Deathgrip on Yesterday....$19.95
00690609 Audioslave $19.95
00690804 Audioslave – Out of Exile $19.95
00690926 Avenged Sevenfold $22.95
00690884 Audioslave – Revelations $19.95
00690820 Avenged Sevenfold – City of Evil....$24.95
00694918 Randy Bachman Collection $22.95
00690366 Bad Company – Original Anthology – Book 1 ....$19.95
00690367 Bad Company – Original Anthology – Book 2 ....$19.95
00690503 Beach Boys – Very Best of $19.95
00694929 Beatles: 1962-1966 ....$24.95
00694930 Beatles: 1967-1970 ....$24.95
00690489 Beatles – 1....$24.95
00694880 Beatles – Abbey Road $19.95
00690110 Beatles – Book 1 (White Album) $19.95
00690111 Beatles – Book 2 (White Album) $19.95
00694832 Beatles – For Acoustic Guitar....$22.95
00690137 Beatles – A Hard Day's Night $16.95
00690482 Beatles – Let It Be $17.95
00694891 Beatles – Revolver $19.95
00694914 Beatles – Rubber Soul $19.95
00694863 Beatles – Sgt. Pepper's Lonely Hearts Club Band ..$19.95
00690383 Beatles – Yellow Submarine....$19.95
00690175 Beck – Odelay $17.95
00690632 Beck – Sea Change $19.95
00694884 Best of George Benson....$19.95
00692385 Chuck Berry....$19.95
00690835 Billy Talent....$19.95
00690879 Billy Talent II $19.95
00690149 Black Sabbath $14.95
00690901 Best of Black Sabbath $19.95
00690148 Black Sabbath – Master of Reality $14.95
00690142 Black Sabbath – Paranoid $14.95
00692200 Black Sabbath – We Sold Our Soul for Rock 'N' Roll $19.95
00690674 blink-182....$19.95
00690389 blink-182 – Enema of the State $19.95
00690831 blink-182 – Greatest Hits....$19.95
00690523 blink-182 – Take Off Your Pants and Jacket $19.95
00690028 Blue Oyster Cult – Cult Classics $19.95
00690851 James Blunt – Back to Bedlam $22.95
00690008 Bon Jovi – Cross Road $19.95
00690913 Boston $19.95
00690932 Boston – Don't Look Back $19.99
00690491 Best of David Bowie....$19.95
00690583 Box Car Racer $19.95
00690873 Breaking Benjamin – Phobia....$19.95
00690764 Breaking Benjamin – We Are Not Alone....$19.95
00690451 Jeff Buckley Collection $24.95
00690678 Best of Kenny Burrell $19.95
00690564 The Calling – Camino Palmero....$19.95
00690261 Carter Family Collection....$19.95
00690293 Best of Steven Curtis Chapman $19.95
00690043 Best of Cheap Trick $19.95
00690171 Chicago – The Definitive Guitar Collection....$22.95
00690567 Charlie Christian – The Definitive Collection $19.95
00690590 Eric Clapton – Anthology $29.95
00692391 Best of Eric Clapton – 2nd Edition....$22.95
00690393 Eric Clapton – Selections from Blues....$19.95
00690936 Eric Clapton – Complete Clapton $29.95
00690074 Eric Clapton – Cream of Clapton $24.95
00690010 Eric Clapton – From the Cradle $19.95
00690716 Eric Clapton – Me and Mr. Johnson....$19.95
00690263 Eric Clapton – Slowhand $19.95
00694873 Eric Clapton – Timepieces $19.95
00694869 Eric Clapton – Unplugged $22.95
00690415 Clapton Chronicles – Best of Eric Clapton $18.95
00694896 John Mayall/Eric Clapton – Bluesbreakers....$19.95
00690162 Best of the Clash $19.95
00690828 Coheed & Cambria – Good Apollo I'm Burning Star, IV, Vol. 1: From Fear Through the Eyes of Madness....$19.95
00690940 Coheed and Cambria – No World for Tomorrow $19.95
00690494 Coldplay – Parachutes $19.95
00690593 Coldplay – A Rush of Blood to the Head $19.95
00690906 Coldplay – The Singles & B-Sides $24.95
00690962 Coldplay – Viva La Vida $19.95
00690806 Coldplay – X & Y $19.95
00690855 Best of Collective Soul $19.95
00690928 Chris Cornell – Carry On $19.95
00694940 Counting Crows – August & Everything After $19.95
00690405 Counting Crows – This Desert Life....$19.95
00694840 Cream – Disraeli Gears $19.95
00690285 Cream – Those Were the Days $17.95
00690352 Creed – My Own Prison....$19.95
00690551 Creed – Weathered $19.95
00690819 Best of Creedence Clearwater Revival....$22.95
00690648 The Very Best of Jim Croce $19.95
00690572 Steve Cropper – Soul Man $19.95
00690613 Best of Crosby, Stills & Nash....$22.95
00690777 Crossfade $19.95
00699521 The Cure – Greatest Hits $24.95
00690637 Best of Dick Dale $19.95
00690882 Dashboard Confessional – Dusk and Summer $19.95
00690892 Daughtry $19.95
00690967 Death Cab for Cutie – Narrow Stairs $22.99
00690822 Best of Alex De Grassi $19.95
00690289 Best of Deep Purple....$17.95
00690784 Best of Def Leppard....$19.95
00694831 Derek and the Dominos – Layla & Other Assorted Love Songs....$22.95
00690384 Best of Ani DiFranco $19.95
00690322 Ani DiFranco – Little Plastic Castle....$19.95
00695382 Very Best of Dire Straits – Sultans of Swing $19.95
00690347 The Doors – Anthology $22.95
00690348 The Doors – Essential Guitar Collection....$16.95
00690915 Dragonforce – Inhuman Rampage $29.95
00690250 Best of Duane Eddy $16.95
00690533 Electric Light Orchestra Guitar Collection $19.95
00690909 Best of Tommy Emmanuel $19.95
00690555 Best of Melissa Etheridge $19.95
00690524 Melissa Etheridge – Skin $19.95
00690496 Best of Everclear $19.95
00690515 Extreme II – Pornograffitti....$19.95
00690810 Fall Out Boy – From Under the Cork Tree $19.95
00690897 Fall Out Boy – Infinity on High $22.95
00690664 Best of Fleetwood Mac $19.95
00690870 Flyleaf $19.95
00690257 John Fogerty – Blue Moon Swamp....$19.95
00690235 Foo Fighters – The Colour and the Shape $19.95
00690808 Foo Fighters – In Your Honor $19.95
00690595 Foo Fighters – One by One....$19.95
00690394 Foo Fighters – There Is Nothing Left to Lose $19.95
00690805 Best of Robben Ford $19.95
00690842 Best of Peter Frampton $19.95
00690734 Franz Ferdinand....$19.95
00694920 Best of Free $19.95
00690222 G3 Live – Joe Satriani, Steve Vai, and Eric Johnson $22.95
00694807 Danny Gatton – 88 Elmira St $19.95
00690438 Genesis Guitar Anthology $19.95
00690753 Best of Godsmack $19.95
00120167 Godsmack $19.95
00690848 Godsmack – IV $19.95
00690338 Goo Goo Dolls – Dizzy Up the Girl....$19.95
00690576 Goo Goo Dolls – Gutterflower $19.95
00690773 Good Charlotte – Chronicles of Life and Death $19.95
00690601 Good Charlotte – The Young and the Hopeless $19.95
00690117 John Gorka Collection $19.95
00690591 Patty Griffin – Guitar Collection $19.95
00690114 Buddy Guy Collection Vol. A-J....$22.95
00694854 Buddy Guy – Damn Right, I've Got the Blues $19.95
00690697 Best of Jim Hall $19.95
00690840 Ben Harper – Both Sides of the Gun $19.95
00694798 George Harrison Anthology $19.95
00690778 Hawk Nelson – Letters to the President $19.95
00692930 Jimi Hendrix – Are You Experienced? $24.95
00692931 Jimi Hendrix – Axis: Bold As Love $22.95
00690304 Jimi Hendrix – Band of Gypsys....$22.95
00690321 Jimi Hendrix – BBC Sessions $22.95
00690608 Jimi Hendrix – Blue Wild Angel $24.95
00694944 Jimi Hendrix – Blues $24.95
00692932 Jimi Hendrix – Electric Ladyland $24.95
00690602 Jimi Hendrix – Smash Hits....$19.95
00690017 Jimi Hendrix – Woodstock....$24.95
00690843 H.I.M. – Dark Light $19.95
00690869 Hinder – Extreme Behavior $19.95
00660029 Buddy Holly $19.95
00660169 John Lee Hooker – A Blues Legend $19.95
00694905 Howlin' Wolf $19.95
00690692 Very Best of Billy Idol....$19.95
00690688 Incubus – A Crow Left of the Murder....$19.95
00690457 Incubus – Make Yourself....$19.95
00690544 Incubus – Morningview $19.95
00690136 Indigo Girls – 1200 Curfews $22.95
00690790 Iron Maiden Anthology....$24.95
00690887 Iron Maiden – A Matter of Life and Death $24.95
00690730 Alan Jackson – Guitar Collection....$19.95
00694938 Elmore James – Master Electric Slide Guitar $19.95
00690652 Best of Jane's Addiction $19.95
00690721 Jet – Get Born $19.95
00690684 Jethro Tull – Aqualung....$19.95
00690647 Best of Jewel $19.95
00690898 John 5 – The Devil Knows My Name $22.95
00690959 John 5 – Requiem $22.95
00690814 John 5 – Songs for Sanity $19.95
00690751 John 5 – Vertigo....$19.95
00694912 Eric Johnson – Ah Via Musicom....$19.95
00690660 Best of Eric Johnson $19.95
00690845 Eric Johnson – Bloom $19.95
00690169 Eric Johnson – Venus Isle $22.95
00690846 Jack Johnson and Friends – Sing-A-Longs and Lullabies for the Film Curious George $19.95
00690271 Robert Johnson – The New Transcriptions....$24.95
00699131 Best of Janis Joplin....$19.95
00690427 Best of Judas Priest $19.95
00690651 Juanes – Exitos de Juanes $19.95
00690277 Best of Kansas $19.95
00690742 The Killers – Hot Fuss $19.95
00690888 The Killers – Sam's Town $19.95
00690504 Very Best of Albert King $19.95
00690444 B.B. King & Eric Clapton – Riding with the King ..$19.95
00690134 Freddie King Collection $19.95
00690339 Best of the Kinks $19.95
00690157 Kiss – Alive! $19.95

FOR MORE INFORMATION, SEE YOUR LOCAL MUSIC DEALER,
OR WRITE TO:

HAL•LEONARD®
CORPORATION
7777 W. BLUEMOUND RD. P.O. BOX 13819 MILWAUKEE, WI 53213

Complete songlists and more at **www.halleonard.com**
Prices, contents, and availability subject to change without notice.

0109

HAL•LEONARD GUITAR PLAY•ALONG

This series will help you play your favorite songs quickly and easily. **INCLUDES TAB** Just follow the tab and listen to the CD to hear how the guitar should sound, and then play along using the separate backing tracks. Mac or PC users can also slow down the tempo without changing pitch by using the CD in their computer. The melody and lyrics are included in the book so that you can sing or simply follow along.

VOL. 1 – ROCK	00699570 / $16.99	VOL. 45 – TV THEMES	00699718 / $14.95
VOL. 2 – ACOUSTIC	00699569 / $16.95	VOL. 46 – MAINSTREAM ROCK	00699722 / $16.95
VOL. 3 – HARD ROCK	00699573 / $16.95	VOL. 47 – HENDRIX SMASH HITS	00699723 / $17.95
VOL. 4 – POP/ROCK	00699571 / $16.99	VOL. 48 – AEROSMITH CLASSICS	00699724 / $14.95
VOL. 5 – MODERN ROCK	00699574 / $16.99	VOL. 49 – STEVIE RAY VAUGHAN	00699725 / $16.95
VOL. 6 – '90s ROCK	00699572 / $16.99	VOL. 50 – NÜ METAL	00699726 / $14.95
VOL. 7 – BLUES	00699575 / $16.95	VOL. 51 – ALTERNATIVE '90s	00699727 / $12.95
VOL. 8 – ROCK	00699585 / $14.95	VOL. 52 – FUNK	00699728 / $14.95
VOL. 9 – PUNK ROCK	00699576 / $14.95	VOL. 54 – HEAVY METAL	00699730 / $14.95
VOL. 10 – ACOUSTIC	00699586 / $16.95	VOL. 55 – POP METAL	00699731 / $14.95
VOL. 11 – EARLY ROCK	00699579 / $14.95	VOL. 56 – FOO FIGHTERS	00699749 / $14.95
VOL. 12 – POP/ROCK	00699587 / $14.95	VOL. 57 – SYSTEM OF A DOWN	00699751 / $14.95
VOL. 13 – FOLK ROCK	00699581 / $14.95	VOL. 58 – BLINK-182	00699772 / $14.95
VOL. 14 – BLUES ROCK	00699582 / $16.95	VOL. 59 – GODSMACK	00699773 / $14.95
VOL. 15 – R&B	00699583 / $14.95	VOL. 60 – 3 DOORS DOWN	00699774 / $14.95
VOL. 16 – JAZZ	00699584 / $15.95	VOL. 61 – SLIPKNOT	00699775 / $14.95
VOL. 17 – COUNTRY	00699588 / $15.95	VOL. 62 – CHRISTMAS CAROLS	00699798 / $12.95
VOL. 18 – ACOUSTIC ROCK	00699577 / $15.95	VOL. 63 – CREEDENCE CLEARWATER REVIVAL	00699802 / $16.99
VOL. 19 – SOUL	00699578 / $14.95	VOL. 64 – THE ULTIMATE OZZY OSBOURNE	00699803 / $16.99
VOL. 20 – ROCKABILLY	00699580 / $14.95	VOL. 65 – THE DOORS	00699806 / $16.99
VOL. 21 – YULETIDE	00699602 / $14.95	VOL. 66 – THE ROLLING STONES	00699807 / $16.99
VOL. 22 – CHRISTMAS	00699600 / $15.95	VOL. 67 – BLACK SABBATH	00699808 / $16.99
VOL. 23 – SURF	00699635 / $14.95	VOL. 68 – PINK FLOYD – DARK SIDE OF THE MOON	00699809 / $16.99
VOL. 24 – ERIC CLAPTON	00699649 / $16.95	VOL. 69 – ACOUSTIC FAVORITES	00699810 / $14.95
VOL. 25 – LENNON & McCARTNEY	00699642 / $14.95	VOL. 71 – CHRISTIAN ROCK	00699824 / $14.95
VOL. 26 – ELVIS PRESLEY	00699643 / $14.95	VOL. 72 – ACOUSTIC '90S	00699827 / $14.95
VOL. 27 – DAVID LEE ROTH	00699645 / $16.95	VOL. 74 – PAUL BALOCHE	00699831 / $14.95
VOL. 28 – GREG KOCH	00699646 / $14.95	VOL. 75 – TOM PETTY	00699882 / $16.99
VOL. 29 – BOB SEGER	00699647 / $14.95	VOL. 76 – COUNTRY HITS	00699884 / $14.95
VOL. 30 – KISS	00699644 / $14.95	VOL. 78 – NIRVANA	00700132 / $14.95
VOL. 31 – CHRISTMAS HITS	00699652 / $14.95	VOL. 80 – ACOUSTIC ANTHOLOGY	00700175 / $19.95
VOL. 32 – THE OFFSPRING	00699653 / $14.95	VOL. 81 – ROCK ANTHOLOGY	00700176 / $19.95
VOL. 33 – ACOUSTIC CLASSICS	00699656 / $16.95	VOL. 82 – EASY SONGS	00700177 / $12.95
VOL. 34 – CLASSIC ROCK	00699658 / $16.95	VOL. 83 – THREE CHORD SONGS	00700178 / $12.95
VOL. 35 – HAIR METAL	00699660 / $16.95	VOL. 96 – THIRD DAY	00700560 / $14.95
VOL. 36 – SOUTHERN ROCK	00699661 / $16.95	VOL. 97 – ROCK BAND	00700703 / $14.95
VOL. 37 – ACOUSTIC METAL	00699662 / $16.95	VOL. 98 – ROCK BAND	00700704 / $14.95
VOL. 38 – BLUES	00699663 / $16.95		
VOL. 39 – '80s METAL	00699664 / $16.95		
VOL. 40 – INCUBUS	00699668 / $16.95		
VOL. 41 – ERIC CLAPTON	00699669 / $16.95		
VOL. 42 – CHART HITS	00699670 / $16.95		
VOL. 43 – LYNYRD SKYNYRD	00699681 / $17.95		
VOL. 44 – JAZZ	00699689 / $14.95		

Prices, contents, and availability subject to change without notice.

FOR MORE INFORMATION, SEE YOUR LOCAL MUSIC DEALER, OR WRITE TO:

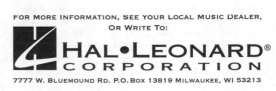

HAL•LEONARD® CORPORATION
7777 W. BLUEMOUND RD. P.O. BOX 13819 MILWAUKEE, WI 53213

Complete song lists available online.

Visit Hal Leonard online at www.halleonard.com